The

Writings

Of

John. K. Whaley

An

Aenigmaticus

Soul

Dedicated to

Sunshine

You started my dreams again and touched the imagination of my soul. I thank you for being a part of my world, and the dreams that are in it. You will be in my heart always.

Contents

Inside one's soul there lays the last frontier of unfound worlds, dimensions, and dreams, the creation of oneself, and all that is to be or could be the imagination, never stop dreaming.

Definition of a Poem

A poem is a living, breathing testament to Humanities inner soul.
Conceived in passion; moments of glory; from valleys of depression and
euphoric highs.

A poem is its own affidavit, standing on its merit. Its validity is in the
mind of the writer, and to the enjoyment of the reader.

J.K.W.

The Beginning

Time fades from the distant past

A new dawn one hopes will last

Reborn to chances given only once, not so it would seem

lest I wake to the same old dreams

Blinded once long ago

Now I've learned to see through the shadow

The spirits of the past I've put behind me

So too the chains that used to bind me

Slowly I will walk upon this earth

Staying true to my rebirth

J.K.W.

GODS

GREED

And Politics

Oh my

1964

In our days of ill spent youth

While we sat searching for the truth

We wore our locks in funny braids

And longed for freedom in strange parades

As others died on distant shores

We lay as barricades in-front of Government doors

And could not see the bloodshed truth

As we quickly lost our hollowed youth

And in doing so we changed the truth

J.K.W.

Lost Paradise

I thought to myself where did paradise go

Lost to evils delusions we did not know

Charlatans and Mystics held us in aw with their endless babble we were enchanted by their call

They promised us prosperity and streets paved with gold

A better life or so we were told

But not soon enough their delusions began to crumble and fold

And still, some could not see evils foot hold

Is it too late, have we lost paradise

Has freedom been sold and what was the price

J.K.W.

The Wolves

Some are like cattle

And some are like sheep

They follow the wolves; whose souls they aim to keep

They wander in the fields mindless and alone

Not knowing that their destiny should be theirs alone not controlled by shadows of the night

Or by mindless howls that aim to fright

Lost and adrift in the blackest night

Never turning their heads to the dawn and the light

For some are cattle and some are sheep

Mooing and baying and weeping in their sleep

J.K.W.

MONUMENTS TO DUST

Ever expanding bridges span

As monuments to the builder man

Giant skyscrapers silhouette this land

All to the glory of the builder man

Highways and byways and freeways do stand

All for the delight of the builder man

Diamonds and silver and trinkets of gold we hold in our hands

All for the greed of the builder man

All the achievements that man has made

Yet how great the price he's paid

The forests, oceans, and the air we breathe

Lost to his own greed

J.K.W.

To the Gods

To the Gods that make us mortals cry

As they look down upon the earth and watch us mortals try

As the days, months and years go by

Surely, they could do more instead of watching us cry

But then I guess that's why they are Gods, and we are but mere reflections in their eyes

J.K.W.

The Board

The board is set, and the game is played

The players assume the moves to be made

One follows the rules that have been given

And one that too; his opponents' intention

But then there are moves that are made that have no direction

To the meaning of which there is no detection

And before you know it, the Gods have set your fate

First its check; and then checkmate

J.K.W.

Frogs

Pollywogs

And other Scary Things

The Frog

The Gods must be angry, I said to myself as I looked toward the darken
sky and watched lighting strike the earth nearby

I felt the rain begin to fall and heard the wind as it began to howl and
thought Lord, I wish I had a towel

Now higher the water began to rise so I said to myself, somewhat
surprised

In a moment I'll have to float it looks like now I'll need a boat

So, I grabbed a passing log that was occupied by a giant bullfrog

and stated quite out loud, why am I sharing this log with this green
bullfrog

The frog did not answer as I expected so I kicked him on his backside
that sent him ejected

It was then that my log began to sink for it was quite hollow and had
sprung a leak right where that bullfrog kept his slimy webbed feet

So, the next time you're up to your nick in the flood, and you find
yourself sharing your log

Don't be so quick to get rid of that green bullfrog

J.K.W.

Pollywogs

I remember the first time I saw a tub full of Pollywogs

And wondered how they could ever become frogs

With strange little bodies that had no legs and one long tail

I thought it would be easier for them to change into a whale

But then what did I know I was only a child of seven, and didn't know much about frogs, whales or even Heaven

As the days and weeks went by, I watched their transformation with a careful eye

From Pollywogs to frogs I watched the change and as they did life turned a page

J.K.W.

Epitaph

Of precious time and beauty, be

The elegant grace of the majestic Manatee

Long before man and his boats were water bond

The lakes and rivers were these mermaids' spawning grounds

So gentle her beauty she shares from afar

How appalling to see her beauty cut and scared

To see her numbers, lie in decay

There for the grace God, could this be humankind someday

But how silly for one to think this way

One would hope for earth's inhabitants

That there would be a better, yet another day

Just before time closes that everlasting door

J.K.W.

The Sirens call

The gulls cry as the suffers ride, and the waves crash upon the shore

 In the spray the Sirens play

Calling to the riders once more to stay

In sets of four the waves rise once more

Beckoning to the riders on distant shore

And still the Sirens call, eternal peace ever more

Undaunted one by one the riders mount, and thrust their souls into the deep

Never fearing the Sirens call, whose beauty in time, will have them all

J.K.W.

Illusions of Love

Loss

And letting go

Through the Mist

As I traveled through the fog and mist and my course surely had no twist

Life as I saw it was quite ok

And so, I thought it would always stay

Never looking or even trying to find

A different path to intertwine

But surely as the Fates did play

A different path came my way

One touch of your hand and my journey did change

You make my journey in everyway

Brighter and brighter with each passing

day

J.K.W.

Beauty

Of ageless time and Beauty, be

More than just a haunting memory

The movement of your spiritual grace

Can change the heart and soul of many a face

You are the light that lights up the room

The angel that clams the stormy gloom

Your Beauty transcends that of conceptual wisdom

The aura of your heart and soul is that of quiet optimism

Of ageless time and Beauty

Never changing throughout eternity

J.K.W.

Daydreams

As I sit here in the solitude of my thoughts

I walk with you in mountains and valleys where no one else has walked

We lay in streams of enchanted bliss

In tranquil succession we would reminisce of days long since past

Of moments we've cherished and the dreams we hoped would last

I would hold you close as the Sun went down

And have vision of you in a silk white gown

With baby's breath upon your head

I would whisper vows never said

As the nightingale would sing

I would give you devotions golden ring

As I sit in here lost in the solitude of my thoughts

Only then do I walk with you

Where no one else could walk

J.K.W.

Bonded

You build your dreams on hopes and fears

Together you share your silent tears

In thoughts and deeds, you try

You hold them together as the seasons pass by

Bonded by more than just a gold ring

For your strength is in the Love you bring

There are days of trouble and days of good

But you face them together as you should

When it's all over and the seasons have ceased

And there is nothing left but eternal peace

And our lives blood no longer flows

I will share my soul with you down Heavens Golden Roads

J.K.W.

Empty

I missed you today

Even though you weren't too far away

I felt you beside me, even though you weren't really there

I could almost touch your cheek as I felt you pass by

You know I missed you today, as I dried a tear from my eye

I could hear your voice as I walked around the house, in all the cracks and corners wherever I stood

I wish I could see your angels face, if only I could

When I stood by the bed, I could swear I felt you reach for my hand

But I guess it was your empty nightstand

I could smell your essence as I lay in our bed

My heart was empty, looking toward the days and nights ahead

J.K.W.

Expressions of Love

I have loved you as the earth has loved her children

I have caressed you like the sea does the shore

I have felt your passion like the winds of a hurricane

I have needed your clam as the fields need the spring rain

I have felt your anger as that of molten lava

I have held your tears like the clouds in the sky

I have felt your fears as tears in my eyes

You are what I touch, what I see, what I smell, even what I taste

You are that which makes me whole

For without you, I am only one part of that which is us

J.K.W.

Friends

Each time I look into your eyes

And caress your curled hair

I think of walks and quiet talks that make me glad you are here

When our fingers touch you hold my heart as you reach forth to hold my hand

And its times like this that ease my mind because you understand

Thus, as the seasons slowly drift and change

And the sun and moon flow with time

My heart will remain ever faithful

To our friendship yours and mine

J.K.W.

Heart and Soul

In my life of all the Loves I have known and lost

Of Hearts and Souls, I thought were truest

Your Heart and Soul was, is and always will be the purest

Even now as the threads of time are spun

You are and forever will remain the one

One pure Heart one pure Soul

And one gentle touch whispered long ago

J.K.W.

If Love were only a solid thing

If Love were a solid thing

Or picture in a picture frame

Or a piece of food to put in your mouth

Perhaps a twisting road winding north and south

Maybe a good book just taken off the shelf

Or maybe a gift to give to someone else

If Love were only a solid thing

Like new mown grass in early spring

Like the sound of mothers as they sing

Or feeding Doves when they take wing

Perhaps Love is a solid thing

Like holding hands and touching fingers

Or one soft kiss that still does linger

If Love were only a solid thing

J.K.W.

If

If I could not talk, would you speak for me

And

If I could not smile, would you smile for me

And

If I could not see would you look for me

And

If I could not cry, would you tear for me

And

If I could not feel as others feel, would you hold out your hands and touch for me

And

If my thoughts weren't clear, would you clear my mind for me

And

If I could not walk, would you stand by my side and steady me

J.K.W.

Inspiration

What song does the Nightingale sing when the music has left her heart

 What poem can the Poet write if he doesn't know where to start

What picture does the artist paint if he doesn't have the colors

And what dreams can the Dreamer see if he has lost his hold on reality

For in your voice the music sings

And in your heart are the colors that this artist paints

And in your eyes are the dreams that this Dreamer sees

And when there is no resemblance of sanity

You are my hold on reality

J.K.W.

Mirage

Your memory fills a part of me

It's more than a memory should be

In the stillness of the night, the rush of the day

Your essence and passion are with me to stay

I taste the air and feel your presence

I feel the wind and hear your voice

I close my eyes and see your face

You touch my soul, then leave no trace

Your body and spirit are etched within me

Like a mirage, I reach out to touch

Longing to hold your passions rush

You spray me with the mists from your soul

Then burn me with your hells desire

And still your memory pushes me higher

Your memory fills a part of me

That's more than a memory should be

J.K.W.

Love

To feel your warmth beside me

Satisfied with gentle touching

To know that you are mine

And I belong to you

In quiet whispers we speak our thoughts

In motions we plan our dreams

To keep safe our love from strangers' schemes

For I am you and you are me

We are as one, forever being in loves warm and passions fever

Never wanting or needing wants

But only having each other

J.K.W.

Space and Time

Of space and time and moments lost

The emptiness like mornings frost

The sounds I hear and voices calling

The loneliness of silence falling

How one can miss an angel's touch

I close my eyes and think of such

Your breath, your warmouth, your smell

How soon it will return to change the still

It seems like an eternity the time that has gone

But in all reality, it has been much, much to long

I count the moments and wait; and wait, standing in the silence

For it is you and you alone that can change the emptiness

And return my world to normalness

J.K.W.

One Moment in Time

If I could have but one moment in time

It would be candlelight dinner and sweet wine

While sitting by the fireplace with your hand in mine

It would be a long evening's walk, with soft peaceful talks

Warm kisses with the morning sun

And welcomed hugs when the day is done

Or sitting on the couch with your head in my lap

As you drift off for a moments nap

Or counting the gray that appears in your hair

And hearing you say that they're not really there

Just one moment in time, is that not too much to ask

A moment of Love, forever to last

J.K.W.

Prisms

In you the sun does shine

If only in the prisms of my mind

And dreams are still dreamt as the clouds do weep

While one moves slowly through futuristic sleep

Still as the wings of time do change

And one silently begins to cope

Therein lies a tiny spark of hope

That forever pushes on

To caress the sunshine as it breaks through the dawn

And as I climb that secret path where the sun does always shine

I hold you close in those brief moments

If only in the prisms of my mind

J.K.W.

Reflections

When I look into your eyes, I see reflections of me

And with my eyes yours is the only face I see

Your eyes glimmer with passion and love

With a heart that's as vast as the sky above

When we first kissed you lifted my soul

To that place I thought I would never know

In this world we pass through many doors, some of them old and some
of them new

I am thankful that I passed through the door that brought me to you

The moments we spend together, are a mere reflection in time

And the time spent apart seems like an eternity to climb

We walk through this world only once, or so I've been told

And on this walk I will have your hand to hold

J.K.W.

Sorrow

Where do you go when the sun doesn't shine

The songs don't sing, and the poems don't rhyme

What do you do when the earth stands still

And the air doesn't flow so there is always a chill

And how can you smile when there's not one to share

Or give your heart when there's not one to give

Or learn to write if you don't have a pen

Or fall in love if you don't let anyone in

J.K.W.

Shallows of my mind

The leaves fall on the ground

Because you are not around

And sadness it fills the air

I hear you voice calling me

Come, take my heart my soul and we will be free

I see the golden sunshine

I see a love that once was mine

In the spring the Robins sing

Even now she still wares my ring

And sadness it reaches me

In the shallows of my mind

J.K.W.

The Flower

I found a small flower amidst a thousand thorns

And removed it ever so gently so not one petal was torn

I planted it in a special way

And nourished it with love and kindness every day

And wherever I went day or night

I never let that small flower out of my sight

I cheeriest it more than all I possessed

But I never gave my flower a moments rest

 I thought that all my flower would need

Was love and kindness on which to feed

But little did I realize that I took away the space from which she
breathed

Every day that passed the harder I tried

But all I could do was watch my small flower die

As I watched, the tears did flow

For the love I gave smothered her so

For you see, I did not know how to let my flower grow

J.K.W.

The Sumer of "64"

On the summer when I was fifteen, I remember walks on the beach, and
meeting the girl of my dreams

She had dark hair and quiet eyes, a gentle voice with romantic sighs

We walked together hand in hand

And lay together on the sand

I held her close during those star filled nights

As we set our dreams on higher sights

We made promises to the sound of the sea

Of the love I had for her and she for me

We spoke in innocents as lovers often do

And on the winds of summer vowed, our love to renew

The summer came and went, and came again

And with it went the promises like the changing winds

Now I sit here and reminisce

I will always be thankful for that summer, and innocents first

kiss

J.K.W.

The Kiss

A once stolen kiss of long ago

Started a slow burning flame from inside my soul

The warmth of your hand as it touched my heart

Brings forth the flame that your shadow does spark

When I look into your eyes, I see the gateway to your soul

You are but one half of the fire

The half that makes us whole

J.K.W.

The Package

I found a package in a quiet place, and went to reach inside

And when I did the miracles, I found were miracles not to hide

These gifts I touched meant so much to what I felt inside me

I brought them forth one by one for all the world to see

They were gifts of love, hope and honesty, of never changing reality

Gifts of patience, trust, and peaceful serenity

All these miracles I hold so true

Are found in that package, that I call you

J.K.W.

These Times

Its times like these I value most

The quiet sharing times, which make us ever close

A touch a glance an unheard thought

A gentle moment that passes not

The words we don't have to say

For we carry them in our hearts every day

Moments spent away from you never seem to pass

And the one's we share together never seem to last

Even as the days and nights slip quietly away

The times we spend together are safe deep within my soul forever to stay

J.K.W.

Thoughts of Love

On thoughts of love and what it should be

Why ask a silly Dreamer such as me

Of knights in shining armor, and fireworks in the sky

I can only venture to guess, and tell you the thoughts from my hearts eye

For you see I've have always thought Love should be a feeling given immeasurably

No strings are chains, or walls of dust

Nothing to hold it in or keep it out

Love is something you cannot see

But you know it's right when it comes to be

Sometimes I think we expect too much

Never realizing that Love is a soft-spoken word, or feathered touch

Then I guess if there are no fireworks, what can I say

You'll have to ask me about love on a rainbow filled day

But these are days few and far between

Somewhat like Love and this Dreamers dreams

J.K.W.

Three words

An angel once said three words to me

Then spread her wings and flew off to be free

And somewhere in flight stole my soul from me

As I watched her ascend into the sky

I wiped two small tears from my eye

One for her and one for the days gone by

One remembers the days and nights we spent together, as higher she flew

We whispered these three words I love you

And as we did the dawn broke through the night

To silhouette her passing flight

Even as the sun began to fade away

There will be memories of better days

Perhaps while visions of the past I see

My angel will return and say those three words to me

J.K.W.

To You

Lines have been written and words have been said

About thoughts of you running through my head

I tried to write these lines, with seductive passions rimes

I thought long and hard about the words to write

Warm and colorful words that would send your heart into flight

Words of magic and loves sweet seduction

But each line I wrote went off in the wrong direction

I thought of the Great Poets and Dreamers, of the Masters past and present

But even then, the words would not come

Only the essences of your sweet kiss still moist upon my lips

I looked for ideas old and new

While still holding images of you

But I guess I should stop and just say what you already knew

These words, I Love you

J.K.W.

Fate
And the
Journey

Journeys End

One travels down many roads on their life's journey never knowing the final destination

We accept our course and the paths we take sometimes without hesitation

Though we think we have all the answers and a road map to show the way

One does not control the fates that often send us astray

I have traveled down a long twisting path, as the fates would attest

Never knowing when are where, are even how my soul would rest

With each step I take I realize that this life is just a test

Always searching for answers from the great cosmic mist

Hoping from the void there would be a list

But as fate would have it no list would be found

So, we continue our journey not knowing where or when our destination comes around

J.K.W.

Journeys Change

I was on a quest I knew not where; I felt a whisper brush against my shoulder and change the journey ever so slightly

Not knowing where the whisper led I chose to travel straight ahead

I thought I heard my name as I turned to walk away

It must have been a passing cloud, to that moment I thought to stay

Perhaps it was only the distant echoes of lost memories that clouded the journeys way

J.K.W.

Out of the Void

I float suspended in time and space

Drifting alone in this tranquil place

Sounds of peace and shapeless thought

Run through my mind I know from not

What is this strength that holds me still

And gives my soul its timeless fill

Forever in darkness shall I be

Trapped in its totality

Suddenly a wave I feel

One of whispers and calm shall steal

Thrust forward with such a force, into a new world I know not its course

Perhaps a vision I had in my first resting place

Will change the journey in my new time and space

J.K.W.

It spins

Around the world and back again

From friends to lovers to friends there in

Like twisting tops and merry-go rounds

You can't stop the spinning for the ups and downs

You run through the labyrinth with no road map in hand

You look for signals to catch as catch can

Just when you think your destination is straight

You see in your path an unopened gate

So, you stop to look for a different path to take

And while you do so, you just sit and wait

Hoping tomorrow the path will be clear and straight

But then you realize it's all just fate

J.K.W.

The Street

I walked down a one-way street

And felt the cobblestone beneath my feet

And wondered as I walked along

Where the cobblestones had first come from

As I stood with that on my mind

My thoughts slowly drifted back in time

To the masons who laid their bricks to native rhymes

Oh, the songs that were sung and the stones that were laid

For the enchanted streets and pathways made

Down twisting roads and winding street

The quiet beauty found beneath our feet

Yet sadly as we look around

So little of that cobblestone can be found

For the roads are pavement bound

No more the beauty or enchantment be, or rhymes or songs of mystery

Somewhere in those cobblestones we lost a part of Orlando's history

J.K.W.

Change

In the quiet waking hours while the dew is still on the ground

We sometimes take for granted as we walk along

The blessings that are given, like the players song

The trees in the forest or the crashing of the waves on distant shore

So go the winds and seasons, still much more

We think that things will never change

As time goes by not to rearrange

But so goes the night and too the sunrise

And the blessings become as tear drops in our minds eye

Somewhere as we walk along, we sadly hear a familiar song, and quietly we hum along

But all too soon the song is gone

J.K.W.

Chance Meetings

Some-times when we walk a strange new course

We don't know which is worse

The longing and waiting or the hunger and thirst

But then the paths we choose to walk aren't randomly laid before us

Yet in the vast eternity, that in all his wisdom man cannot really see

The paths we choose to walk were laid a thousand years before thee

And if one walks slowly and looks in both directions

He catches a glimpse of other highways, and hollow streets of lost shallow reflections

For only time knows the paths we take and the roads that one travels down

And at the crest of every street surely lies a quiet tranquil town

J.K.W.

Family

Tribute to Mom

This one's for you

You were there when I fell and busted my chin

You opened your arms and let your love come in

You were there through my nightmares

And down through the years, you were there to wipe away my tears

You were there to make me warm when I was cold

And there to cool me down when I was hot

You were there during the highs and lows of my life

You taught me, love and understanding

You were there when I needed a friend

This one's for you, you gave me something no one else could

You taught me life and how to live

J.K.W.

The Siblings

Sometime as the sun came up

I thought of spring and Daffodils, Tulips and Butter Cups

I saw the wagons on parade

And remembered as children how we dressed up and played

I laugh when I think of us back then

But it makes me warm when my mind drifts back now and again

I can see us as if it were yesterday

The three musketeers lost in magical play

But then my thoughts drift back to today only to steal me away, from those three children lost in magical play

Yet as I look into our eyes

I can still drift back to those times

When our world was new, as we were too

J.K.W.

The Hug

Daddy, can I have a hug she said to me

I said sure, is something troubling you

She said no, not particularly

So, I gave her a hug and a great big squeeze

And thanked the Lord for moments like these

For all too often in our busy days

The moments pass in subtle ways

And little hugs disappear with the evenings haze

So, like the evening the morning slips away

And all too soon we will long for the days

Before we lost our moments to yesterday

Daddy, can I have a hug

J.K.W.

Sleep now my children

Sleep now my children and dream your dreams

Ride the clouds on Pegasus's wings

Build crystal castles and diamonds in the sand

Rings of gold to hold in your hand

Ride the winds of time, and swim the seas, and think of kaleidoscope fantasies

Sleep now my children dream long and true

Dream of things old and new

The mountains and valleys, and rivers of gold

Keep them in your hearts forever to hold

J.K.W.

Solemn Faces

The children sit with solemn faces

Who will be there when the tears start to fall

To wipe them dry so no one can tell

That their parents put them through their thoughtless hell

And who will make it all right again

Neither the King nor all the Kings men

For no one can see what goes on inside

Those unholy fears that little children hide

Their world torn apart at the seams

And still, no one can hear their inward screams

For we as foolish parents wonder

And then we blame each other for the others blunder

And try as one might to change the tide

All efforts push their fears deeper inside

And no one will see the damage that's been done

Until it comes back to haunt them one by one

J.K.W.

Silent Questions

As the Angels sing, so goes the clouds

We done are mists in quiet shrouds

On owls wings we hear no sound

In the echo of the thunder our tears touch the ground

To our rage we turn away, and think of passions turned to clay

As children we thought a new; to open doors once passed through

Each door we opened shut within our own lost silence that has never been

In strange disguise we try to hide

The essence of this madness once satisfied

Ensign, we try to speak, only to receive silence to answers we seek

J.K.W.

Rebellion

An angry young man I stood, in defiance of Parenthood

Thoughts of rebellion running through my mind

When my Elders were just trying to be kind

And teach me the wisdom that they have gained down through the years

And all I could do was give them tears

Like gentle words spoken but never heard

The silence went through my every nerve

To myself I thought what do they know

Am I not young, and they very old

With the circle of time, my thoughts have changed

And their wisdom is mine to exchange

With another young man who's thoughts are enraged, with thoughts of rebellion as we turn the page

J.K.W.

Never a Man

My little brother I hear you call

My little brother my you've grown tall

My little brother it's now that you are talking

My little brother now you are walking

People are talking they don't understand

My little brother will never be a man

J.K.W.

Letting Go

I looked at you today, and felt you slipping away

A tear rolled down my cheek when I knew you weren't looking

I thought of times when I held you close

And I thought then of how you loved me the most

But looking at you now I see, a different you and a changing me

You've lost that look of innocence and replaced it with a sassy smile

That in a few short years will drive all the young men wild

But just remember as you journey through time

A short call to Dad will give peace of mind

J.K.W.

Grandfathers House

There stands an old white blockhouse on an acre of ground

Where sometimes old voices can be heard, and peaceful memories abound

Whereas a child, my Grandfather and I, through our dinner window would watch the quail pass by

And where on summer mornings and quiet afternoons, I would spend my time dreaming and whistling crazy tunes

Where Grandfather would tell me stories of days gone by

Some would make you laugh, and some would make you cry

I learned a lot from my Grandfather in the days of my youth

Of life and love and the words of truth

The old house still stands

Yet somewhat different from when I played there in my youth

But I still go back there every now and again

To dream and seek the truth

And remember where it all began, those days of my youth and the foundation on which it stands

J.K.W.

Funky Winker Bean

I carried you when you could not walk

I spoke for you when you could not talk

I held you up when you tried to walk and coached you when you started
to talk

I was there for your first fight, and told you that your lip would be all
right

I picked you up when you fell off your bike

And knew if I left you alone you would get it right

I tried to guide you through your course in life

In hopes to save you from some of the journey's strife

And in doing so I may not have always got it right

I tried to do the best I could as any parent might

I hope it's understood, I tried to teach you Love, respect and
Brotherhood

J.K.W

City under the house

Oh, Grand City of many-colored lights

Of golden roads and crystal-colored nights

Filled with illusions and kaleidoscope dreams

Consecrated columns filled with little boys' schemes

Where the silhouettes of fantasy would become an ever-changing reality

Yes, underneath that old house where one used to play, and build his visions from earth and clay

From which the foundation of reality was laid, and the visions of many a story were made

One must go back there every once and awhile, if only to dream and ponder a smile

If only to think of what used to be, those forgotten days in youthful fantasy

J.K.W.

Cherished Gifts

Oh, the games we as parents play

We don't see the consequences of another day

Take heed in these words I write

Should you lose your dreams to judgments might

For what dreams are given; can always be taken away

For dreams are here for just a short stay

They are gifts to be cherished every day

Not to be used in whimsical way

J.K.W.

Spirituality

Angels in the wind

Entrusted to us as Angels in the wind are Gods precious seeds the souls of his children

They are given to us only on loan

These seeds who's fruit are not our own

If you take the seeds and plant them right

And nourish them with a guiding light

With hope and love, joy and peace, faith, and discipline and so much more than these

You watch them mature and slowly grow

These precious seeds that God did sow

As Angles in the wind, they are given to us, with God's love we eternally trust to guide them until their journeys end

These seeds that are scattered as Angels in the wind

J.K.W.

Dark Woods and Whispering Winds

I traveled down an eerie path filled with dark woods and whispering winds

And in the shadows that I saw were the faces of my sins

The further I walked along the weaker my legs became

It was as if I was in quicksand as the faces remained the same

So as my heart began to slow down and somehow my fears began to leave, I put one foot in front of the other with but one mighty giant heave

I eluded shadows along the way, running as fast as my legs could go

Hoping somewhere down the path, I would run into someone I might know

The deeper I ran into the woods my fears began again

When suddenly I saw a light with a gentle hand therein

I reached forth from within the thicket and clutched that hand so tight, and in doing so I found a friend for life, not just for the dark and whispery night

J.K.W.

Eternity

Behind one door there was one more

And behind that one there was another

So, it went from here to there with nothing in-between

Like a thousand nights and thousand days lost in silent dream

The bellmen has the key to all, at least that's how it seems

But if we try, and pay or tithes, to make our reservation now

The keys that are there, will be his to share to each and every door

And there will always be one more; and then again one more

J.K.W.

Faith

I have thought as much as one man could

About life, love, and brotherhood

The why and ways, and asked for guidance from above

And in doing so I took to task

That in my prayers I dared to ask, the question that man dared not dream

The universe its scope, and the Creators grand scheme, of life, love, and brotherhood

I offered incents and sacrificial lamb

In the hope the Creator would take them in hand

So as to help me understand, the whys and the ways of the earthbound man

But who are we to question God

For what he gave to help us understand, is to accept as our savior the Son of man

J.K.W.

Folded Hands

One wishes they could change the day

And somehow turn the night away

And close the doors to evils might

To send adversity from one's sight

Tis hard to conquer these tasks alone

As hard as you try, your efforts are scattered like the oceans foam

One wonders from mountain to valley and back again

But still the night's illusions trickle in

And the mountains you build are departed like the winters wind

One searches for answers within one's own thoughts

Thus, closing the door to answers sought

Never hearing that gentle knock

For the answers you seek open your heart

By putting your hands together, then the knowledge will start

J.K.W.

Food for The Soul

What food the tired soul does need, of bread, wine and meat take heed

These are not the Staff of Life the soul does need

To satisfy your earthly hunger, ingest those things that man has given

Still your pains will not be quelled

For the more you consume the more you desire

Of the soul you ask, then what to feed

The written word is all one needs

In the word is truth, and truth is the Sacrament for which the staving soul does need

In the sacred parchments of Saints and Prophets long since past

Is found the ambrosia, that will forever last

J.K.W.

Have and Have Nots

What if in the land of the melting pot

There were those that have and the have nots

And the ones who have not gave all that they could share

And the ones who have did not; and did not care

So, the Haves got more as time went on

And the Have Nots had less with each new dawn

But on that day when the final morning came, the Haves had only themselves to blame

Yes, it was true they had it all; but they ignored the Teachers call

For the haves to share, you see was simply never done

In the end they lost their souls one by one

What of the Have Nots, they heard the call, and in the end they had it all

J.K.W.

JUDGMENT

What's there to life that you don't understand

Don't you know that greed is the color of man

What's there to tell you what's there to say

Well, we be here come JUDGMENT DAY

When the mountains crumble, when the mountains fall

Will it be the strong or the weak that pay for us all

Who is to decide, who is to say, will it be you or me brother come
JUDGMENT DAY

J.K.W.

Revelation

I dreamed I was dying, and my soul floated away

Somewhere beyond Calvary, so I could not see eternity

As the void of blackness surrounded me

I floated somewhere between time and space

A small ray of light shined on my cheek

Then in my mind the words began to speak

Salvation is the light you seek

I reached forth with my heart toward the light through the dark

And felt a power no mortal could create

A force so great and divine, that its very essence consumed my heart, soul, and mind

Sprit said I, or Creator be, save me from this black hole of eternity

So, as I wept, my fears subsided, and I felt the presence of my Lord beside me

He saved my soul and returned me to Calvary

J.K.W.

Searching for Home

I rode the winds and thought nothing of the power and benevolence from
above

I turned my back to Calvary and lost sight in that he died for me

I gave up on the resurrection and went off in my own direction

To live the life of earthly man and never tried to understand

That Jesus holds us all in the palm of his hands

I tried to make it on my own always looking for a place to call home

When all at once it occurred to me, there is a home in eternity

As I stood there with that on my mind, I opened my soul and let the
Lord entwine

J.K.W.

The Door

A door is a very curious thing

It doesn't say much it just stands in a frame

You open it, you close it

You pass through its dimensions, with great apprehension, wandering what's on the other side

Some doors open into hollow spaces filled with people with empty faces

While others open into cold concrete walls that serve as mankind's punitive halls

Still behind some doors a Lady does stand, who holds the balance of Judgment in her hands

Yet others old and run down open into rooms where knowledge can be found

There are doors of many persuasions, sizes, and shapes

There are doors insides one's mind for which there is no escape

But as we stand upon the threshold there is but one door we must pass through, the young, the old and the brand new, the door that opens to the Promised Land

With the keys that lie in the soul of man

J.K.W.

The Path

I am glad I opened up my heart and let my savior in

For he carried away my burdens and wiped away my sins

Through the constant daily struggle

I will put my trust and faith in him

To bare his stripes and walk his path no matter what the cost

Like a beacon in the night glowing to save the lost

Because long ago on Calvary, he shed his blood for souls like you and
me

Tis a small price to pay for Eternity to walk the path toward Calvary

J.K.W.

The World Revolves Around Itself

Press on as the world revolves around itself

As people pass through revolving doors and stand on escalators instead of floors

Traversing on pathways to unknown lands

Searching for answers without any plans

Not seeing the answers in their outstretched hands

For long ago in a distant land a foundation was laid on which all can stand

With but one request with the folding of hands, accept his promise, and you can walk the path to the Promised Land

On this you have the promise of the Carpenters hands

J.K.W.

Lessons

Lessons

When we think life's to tough

And we finally say enough, is enough

You know when those little things just get you down

And you're really not much fun to be around

Look deep in your heart and see what you can find

Deep, deep in your heart, soul, and mind

Think of those less fortunate than you

The Men, Women and Children whose lives have been torn into

As often as the pages turn, we forget the lessons in life we've learned

We put our needs above the rest and seem to forget that this life is just a
test

J.K.W.

Hold Fast Your Dreams

Hold fast your Dreams never let them die

Take wings and fly across the sky

Hold near your tears catch them as they fall

Hold still you're days and share them with a smile

Hold tight your friends never let them fade

Hold fast your Dreams and share them with us all

For all too soon, dreams die, and tears fall like rain, and your days pass one into the other

Friends surely fade; and through the mists of time, you will walk in your own parade

J.K.W.

Look inside

Who looks inside to see the real me

When the exterior is all that people care to see

It seems that in this supersonic world in which we live

We are all so willing to take but not to give

One looks at the spit and polish, buttons, and bows, never touching the mountains that this soul knows

When the outside is all, you see, you will never know the heart of me

One should take the time to see the foundation on which one stands

To see if that foundation is truth, or just windblown sand

J.K.W.

HOPE

Through the days and nights, we wait

Looking for someplace to escape

Surrounded by haunted dreams we pray

Should shadows in the night steal us away

The dawn awakes us and takes flight

In the hopes to see another light

Still the powers that be sometimes make fools of you and me

Yet in thy sleep and waking hours

We pull the petals from hopes sweet flowers and touch the rainbows
from distant towers

And occasionally plant new seeds to sprout, faith, charity and hopes
sweet flowers

J.K.W.

NEVER too late until the Sunshine Fades

As long as there is a ray of hope; it's never too late

Surely as there is a Heartbeat; it's never too late

As long as ones soul survives; it's never too late

Until the breath of life has left; it's never too late

Even in the twilight of Heaven's gates; it's never too late

When every ray of hope has turned to darkness and there is no more Heartbeat only sadness

Even when the soul has faded into the abyss and the last breath of life has dwindled into the mist

It's never too late until the Sunshine fades

J.K.W.

Ignored

I sat around just twirling my thumbs

Filled with a case of the boring Ho-Hums

As I sat there thinking of something to do

I quite naturally closed my eyes, and proceeded to saw a long into

I could have done a number of different things

Like build a house, write a book, be an engineer on a train or build a
fancy airplane

But I choose to be totally bored

And soon discovered the world chose me to be completely ignored

J.K.W.

REALITY

There is no crystal ball that shows what the future should be

Only that untraveled path of reality

With eyes open we forge ahead

Taking on those tasks that we sometimes dread and in doing so we are better than we once were

Thus, we try to profit by mistakes made and travel new roads that no one else has paved

When at the crossroads of our final years, one hopes we can look back at the past and shed no tears

J.K.W.

ART

A child is like an artist's canvas

And parents are the brushes

So, the strokes we as parents give put color to the canvas

Bold, daring, warm and caring

They can paint love, compassion, and gentle sharing

Or they can be dark, allusive, transparent, even cold, eerie, and
somewhat dreary

But it's up to us to choose our colors right so let's paint our canvases
warm, compassionate, sunny, and bright

J.K.W.

TOMORROW

What good is Poetry if it is not read

What good is art if it's not seen

What good is the play without the Actors

The Rhyme without the reason

The years without the Seasons

Dreams without Reality

Life without Hope

And Hope without Tomorrow

Poetry is read

Art is seen

And the play does have Actors

Rhymes have reason

And the years have Seasons

There is Reality in Dreams

And tomorrow must surely bring hope

At least that's how it would seem

J.K.W.

Serenity

Serenity

The night creatures sang in symphonic harmony

As the twilight falcon directed their perfect symphony

The stars were the brightest I've seen as I lay there in peaceful dream

One could hear the deer as they began to roam

As the night surrounded my country home

I lay there with not a care on my mind

I felt at peace, just passing the time

As I lay surrounded by all this serenity, I felt a dark emptiness from within the heart of me

A loneliness that attacked my very soul, with a grip so strong it would not let go

I ask myself what would make me feel this way, as I listened to the night at play

You see there was nothing I could do

For the darkness and the loneliness, I felt was, not having the Serenity of you

J.K.W.

SOLITUDE

I long to be on distant mountains

Far away from the city lights, with crowded streets and crazy nights

Away from where people are always moving to and fro

Never stopping always on the go

To see and hear the majestic waterfall

To feel the wind and hear the eagles call

To sense and enjoy natures plan

To hold her bosom in my hands

To walk the grand forest far, so too, to see the beauty in the nights flashing stars

To have the sky as my shelter, a thousand miles away from the cities helter-skelter

J.K.W.

THE WALK

To walk among the piney woods and feel the needles beneath my feet

To smell the memories of the forest great and deep

Once more to see the distant smoke of the canons fire, to charge the Castle and never tire

To dig beneath the forests cover, and find its bits of hidden treasure

To hear the quails call, and see the fireflies light, and journey beyond the starlight

To fade into that short night from which dreams have sprung, if only for one last mystic journey and stories once more to come

Like that spirit who haunts the piney woods, sacred as he may be, I once knew his presence as a childes memory

From time to time, every now and then, that spirit finds his way to piney woods every now and again

J.K.W.

LONGING

As I sit here far from home, an image of her face I see

And in my present state of mind, her sweet sleep is calling me

I 'm standing here on this sinking ship, thinking of the times I've had

And in the morning, it will all be over, for it was just a dream gone bad

But, even now as my chest begins to pain and the waters begin to come
over me

I feel the warmth of her sweet sleep and longing, longing to be free

And when the morning finally came, the shadows that were seen, were
the faces of one hundred men lost in eternal dream

J.K.W.

Illusions

And

Shadows in the night

Shadows

In the hidden corners and the passages of our mind

Somewhere between the darkness and the light you will find, deep within the Labyrinth the Shadows reside

The Shadows that haunt us and play with Destiny's fate

So swift and silent their movements, we cannot see until it's too late

Just when you think you are on the right path, that's when the Shadows choose to laugh

So, beware of the Shadows and the roadblocks they throw

The Shadows are there, and now you know, they try to screw with your heart, mind, and soul

J.K.W.

Descended

Too soon the leaves are gone, and the night has turned a page

And we can never change the things we tried to rearrange

Drifting like illusions shadows from the sun, departing into the void now as one

Slowly fading into the day, the shadows transcend away

New forms take shape as clouds in the wind; dreams go as nightmares to return again and again

False hopes and visions echo in our minds, and to soon descend into the void of time

J.K.W.

THE SMOG

I sat in the mist of mass confusion

A prisoner to my own illusion

I looked for the truth and pondered reason

And lost in part the changing seasons

Stagnated did my mind become, lost in eternal boredom

I tried to cling to some form of sanity, yet slipped over the edge of reality

Things in life are not always as they seem, so much they are as changing dreams

J.K.W.

Illusions

Life is not always what it seems

We look at it through transparent dreams

The things we take for granted, like the changing of day are really life's illusions, like the games people play

We think we know what's up and what's down

The things that are square and those that are round

What's forward and what's backward

What's a couch or bed, after all they are no more than illusions inside or head

J.K.W.

Dust by Dawns First Light

The times were once and long ago

Where shadows hid and fields flowed

And dancing fairies with gnomes did play on beds of wild field grass, watching visions of castles and knights go past, or battles of Blue and Gray

Still sometimes seeing dragons fly away

Jumping over the walls of some mysterious foe, then descending to the earth's center below

Once and mighty fields did grow, but my that was long ago

And now the grass is gone, and nothing remains but memories to dream on

J.K.W.

Lost in the Void

Lost

I stood before the fog and haze, my life before lost in a daze

Time stood still; my soul in the labyrinth lost and alone, as if my breath
and being were no longer my own

The pain, the gut-wrenching all-encompassing pain, I felt num and loss
of control

There was nothing no light, my universe now a black hole did consume

I was no one, then everyone

Too many thoughts, so much rain, then the pain, like that of a trillion
Suns, but yet so much cold: cold ever freezing cold

I longed for the Reaper to take my soul and free me from the fog and
haze; he could not find me in this eternal maze

There must be a way back to who I once was, and escape from what I
might become

One second, one minute, one hour, one day, one night, one week, one
month, one year at time

With faith, hope, trust, and love within me, once again my soul will be
free

J.K.W.

I am

I am alone, void of hope, time, and spirit

I am a void in space, a sound and no one can hear it

I am an empty shell on the oceans floor

I am a fleeting moment passing through an unseen door

I am a whisper in the wind, and no one can feel it

I am a shadow which no one can see

I am the soul that's never free

I am a black hole in space without time or dimension

I am lost and alone without acceptation

J.K.W.

Goddess of Tears

I stood before the Goddess of Tears

I bared my soul and all my fears

I held my hand to her breast

And gave this idol my spirit to rest

But the Goddess cried, and gave me back my soul to hide

I thought how kind this Goddess be, at last to set my soul free

But through her eyes the tears still fell, and slowly pulled my soul to Hell

I stood before the Goddess of Tears, never more to bare my soul and all my fears

J.K.W.

Child Dreams

Technicolor Dreams

As children we looked at the world through Technicolor eyes

Exploring each moment with grand surprise

In a world of make believe we would play, taking for granted the changing of the days

In our minds eye we would see, passing moments in ever changing fantasy

Never thinking of what life someday might be

As teens we thought of coming days, and never times spent in childish ways

Our hours were spent on thoughts of change, and the world we just knew that someday we could re-arrange

As adults we all to soon came to be, and lost sight of dreams we once thought we could see

As we grew old and time did pass, we turned back or minds to our childhood days, when we looked at the world through Technicolor eyes, and explored each moment with grand surprise

J.K.W.

Closet

Thump, Thump, Thump

What is that sound I hear, making my heart race, and filling my mind with fear

Should I take a chance and get out of bed, and walk to the corner of my room, and open the door to which I dread

Thump, Thump, Thump, there it goes once more, that sound like nothing I've ever heard before

Is it some Alien from outer space, or a giant rat running a race

Perhaps a six-foot-tall invisible white rabbit, in a funny pink suit, or a mystical storyteller playing a magical flute

Could it be some type of ugly hairy beast, looking for something on which to feast

Thump, Thump, Thump, there it goes again

Now I know I must get up and open the closet door to see what lies therein

So, with great apprehension I threw back my covers and walked ever so slowly toward that closet door, and pushed it open

To find laying on the floor, a fallen toy and nothing more

J.K.W.

The Play Ground

What can be said of swings and things

Merry-go-rounds and monkey rings

Of balance beams and children's dreams

Slides and sand boxes, and magical things

Caterpillars and butterflies, climbing mountains and rolling in the grass
where the valley lies

Touching trees and watching the falling leaves as they hit the ground, or
seeing your youth as they run through a mystical playground

J.K.W.

The Presence of Innocence

I stood in the presence of innocence, and watched in total silence as they played their running games

Somewhere deep inside my soul, I started to feel like that child of long ago

I began to think with unspoken innocence, about an old friend that I have long since missed

I felt his presence inside my heart

So, in my thoughts we began to play, me and my childhood friend of yesterday

We played those games that only children do, and dreamed of adventures, castles, and mystic battles

On magic horses we would ride, through psychedelic clouds

As I looked closer, deep within my thoughts, I began to see my childhood friend looking back at me

J.K.W.

The River through a Childs Eyes

Underneath this concrete and clay, flows a river whereas a child I used to play

One filled with dreams of tomorrow, the hopes of the past and little boys fishing with rods they would cast

There were trips down the Amazon or distant rivers on a planet somewhere in space, and river rafts racing at a frantic pace

The North and the South fighting, or an Olympic race

From narrow streams the water would run, from which childhood dreams were often spun

The drainage ditch still lies where I once washed my hands, and as a young boy I would visit new and distant lands, somewhere just before time, hidden in the rivers of my mind

J.K.W.

THE STALLION

From a time when there was no history

And the secrets of life were shrouded in enchanted mystery

There was born a valiant steed, of ebony color and unmatched speed

An animal of Nobel bravery, and unending deed

With fire in his eyes, and blazing hooves that would gallop across the majestic skies

A magic stallion that even had the Gods beguiled, who carried on his back the hopes and dreams of one small child

No, there has never been a more nobler steed, not of mind or heart or unending deed

Nor has ever loved this child to the depth of his enchanted soul, as that gallant equine with the name Billy Diablo

J.K.W.

The Dreamer

THE DREAMER

Long, long ago in the not-too-distant past, there lived a Magic Dreamer and visions were his task

He'd conjure up illusions of Black Stallions, and Castles in the skies, or silver crested flying things from the twinkle in his eyes

For life was his canvas, and the imagination was his brush, and the artistry that he would dream he'd share with some of us

For in his mind there were many hidden places, of a million dreams, with ever changing faces

Some good, some bad, some with all the colors of the rainbow

Dreams that would make your heartbeat fast, and dreams that would make it beat slow

Dreams of love and sweet seduction, and quiet thoughts of Man and his redemption

Of children playing on merry-go-rounds and shady little roads in quite sleepy towns, of sunlight shining through the windowpane, and wood fairies dancing in the forest rain, and shadows, silhouettes, and dreams not dreamt

At least not to this Dreamer not yet

So as the light years shoot across the skies and one catches the twinkle in the Dreamers eyes, remember the dreams within you that lie, somewhere behind the twinkle in your eyes

J.K.W.

Silhouettes

Locked up inside your mind, if you open your heart you will find, silhouettes, shadows and visions of dreams, the stories, and fantasies that only you can share

Never hold back the stories that you have, the good ones, the bad ones even the sad

J.K.W.

Dust

Slowly but surely, it comes along, that exchange from twilight to dawn that brings out the fairy dust, from which cosmic hopes are spawn, and eternal dreams are drawn

Inside the dust there lives a mystic world of ever-changing mystery, shaping this world's destiny and altering the course of history

Who knows what dreams the dust does show, flowing dreams of love or madness grow from within the twilights dust we do not know

One must watch the dreams as they unfold

Lest we lose the dreams we should ever hold, of medieval castles, and knights of old, enchanted stories never told

J.K.W.

Forest Dreams

In quiet forests I walked in days since gone, strange the dreams I used to creep upon

So many adventures and Dragons slayed, a thousand Kingdoms and Maidens made

I was a Spirit born on the wind

I lived illusions and moments hidden therein

I flew over the Earth and felt her bosom within

I touched the Heavens and cried again, and felt Her pain upon my skin; I saw a cloud with a golden city

A mystical place the forest was; where Dreams, Dragons, Kingdoms, and Maidens were made and so much more, looking up from the Forest floor

J.K.W

What Dreams May Come

What dreams may come, when sleep is not, and time stands alone, like the Pyramids of old

When thoughts like random raindrops fall, too many to decipher

Lest shattered glass splits the mind and dreams escape through the void of time

Once more lost between the sheets of cotton, as past shadows all but forgotten

J.K.W.

Snippets

Snippets:

The only True reality is the reality of Truth itself

Given time one will find the answers to most of the questions, or one will question most of the answers. Therein lies the difference between who leads and who follows.

One should take time to know the Man or Woman, to see if their foundation is Truth or just windblown sand.

Wisdom is that process, which is developed though trail and errs, or when one is very old, he or she is said to be very wise.

When the burner is hot you soon learn not to touch it.

Creativity is only limited to where the imagination takes you, and the resources one has at hand.

Sometimes the enemy is not that which is in front of you, but that which is inside of you.

Do we walk upon this earth, or do we just lift our feet as the world turns beneath us? In essence, do we stand in one place as the world passes us by, or do we walk forward one step at a time?

Time is an illusion; drifting through the void it has no beginning, and no end. There is no today or yesterday or the day after, there is only the now; and that in and of itself is just a phantasm of reality

Definition} Aenigmaticus {Latin} an enigma obscure, Puzzling: enigmatic

J.K.W.

Warning

Last Chance

We stand at the Epoch of a new millennium, in which man controls his own destiny

There is a river of tears from all the Nation's children; for they drown in the blood of their forefathers and their fathers yet to come

The Earth cries and no one hears, she morns the loss of her children

Her blood is rancid with disease, Her heart and arteries are hard from abuse

Her lungs choke with the cancer of Humanity

We stand at the Epoch of a new millennium

God grant us the wisdom and authority to change our destiny

J.K.W.

What Lies Before Us

On his face the scars cut deep

And in his eyes like empty pools of darkness did show, hidden fears
from generations' tears of ten-thousand years in mourn

His huddled mass now shriveled and torn stands as testimony to warn,
the next generations coming tears, and hopes that Humanity will cleanse
his fears, and save us all from the coming years

J.K.W.

Rust

One remembers when parks and forests used to abound

And all you could hear was laughter and see children on swings and merry-go-rounds

When the grass was green and lakes were clear, and an abundance of life did abide in there

When the sky was blue as the clouds floated by, and Eagles separated earth and sky

Then quietly like the fresh spring rain, the land was stripped to make way for growing pains

Slowly the construction went up without much fuss, with an array of buildings to shelter all of us

As we watched in Apathy, the parks and forests turned to dust; and then our sacred castles crumbled to rust

J.K.W

Epilogue

Some Dreams are made for Dreamers

Some Dreamers make their own Dreams

Some Dreams become reality

And some Dreams just fade into obscurity

But one must never give up on dreams

For Dreams create Hope and through Hope, is created the future and with the future the circle continues, beyond the next Generation, to the next and so on…………………..